Experienci

Solomon Hailu, PhD.

Table of Contents

Preface

The ministry of the Holy Spirit is active today. The Holy Spirit never stopped distributing His gifts to empower believers. The purpose of this book is to demonstrate my personal experiences with the gifts of the Spirit. Every believer has received a gift from the Holy Spirit. The Bible confirms that fact when it says, "…you will receive the gift of the Holy Spirit. The promise is for you and your children and for all who are far off—for all whom the Lord our God will call" (Acts 2.39). But only those who unwrap the gift would know what kind of gift(s) he or she has received. So, have you opened the gifts and enjoyed them yet? If not, it is time to unwrap the package! Do not wait any longer. It is time to rediscover what is in store for you. The apostle Paul reminded his spiritual son, Timothy, not to neglect the Spiritual gifts (1 Timothy 4:14). He encouraged him to rather stir up the gifts (2 Timothy 1:6).

Chapter One: The Origin of the Gifts

To fully understand the gifts of the Spirit and how they operate, one must first know their origin. The Bible tells that the giver of the gifts is the Holy Spirit: "There are different kinds of gifts, but the same Spirit distributes them" (1 Corinthians12:4).

Therefore, it is so important that we establish a relationship with the giver (the Holy Spirit) prior to seeking His gifts. When the Holy Spirit is put first, the gifts will follow normally. Smith Wigglesworth said, "Wherever the Holy Spirit has the right of way, the gifts of the Spirit will be in manifestation; and where these gifts are never in manifestation, I question whether he is present."

The Lord Jesus Christ Himself began His earthly ministry only after the Holy Spirit came upon Him at the Jordan River (Matthew 3:16). Jesus acknowledged the fact that His ministry was driven by the power of the Holy Spirit from beginning to end. At the onset of His ministry, Jesus declared, "The Spirit of the Lord is on me, because He has anointed me" (Luke 4:18). Jesus received power from the Holy Spirit to cast out the devil, to heal the sick (Luke 4:18), to preach the good news (Luke 4:18). Jesus went on the cross with the power of the Holy Spirit (Hebrew 9:14). Jesus was raised from the dead by the Holy Spirit (Acts 8:1). He ascended to heaven by the power of the Holy Spirit, and the cloud received Him (Acts 1:9). He will return by the power of the Holy Spirit: "He is coming with the clouds (Revelation 1:17). Clearly, the Holy Spirit has been at the center of the ministry of Jesus.

Therefore, it is quintessential that we receive power from the Holy Spirit before we enter the ministry. To put ministry before the Holy Spirit is putting the cart before the horse. That is not the right order. Jesus is our extraordinary model in the ministry. We should learn from Jesus, who is the author and finisher of our faith. If our Lord Jesus Christ, the Son of almighty God, was entirely dependent upon the power of the Holy Spirit, how much more His followers should rely upon the anointing and power of the Holy Spirit to have success in ministry.

Nowadays, the church appears to be more of a religious institution rather than God's powerhouse. It has formal administrative and leadership structures, but the power of the Holy Spirit is missing. Most churches are like a bus full of people with the driver sitting behind the wheel, but the bus is not moving, so people start to step out of the bus because it does not get them anywhere. Who would want to sit in an unmovable bus for a whole day? The number of church goers dwindles every week because people are not getting something worth their time and money.

The Church needs to reestablish its relationship with the Holy Spirit all over again, and should give the Holy Spirit the right of way. One of the secrets of the great evangelist Kathryn Kuhlman's successful ministry was giving special priority to the Holy Spirit. She was often heard saying, "Please do not offend my friend. He is here." She pleaded with the great crowd of people to welcome the Holy Spirit before their needs. She had the practice of spending hours and hours praising and worshiping the Holy

Spirit in front of the great crowd. The Holy Spirit in return honored that and conspicuously released His supernatural gifts during her services.

The Lord Jesus Christ instructed His disciples to wait for the same Holy Spirit that helped Him throughout His ministry (Acts 1:4-5). The Holy Spirit was dispensed for the first time on the day of Pentecost (Acts 2:1), and here we see that the disciples received the Holy Spirit before beginning their ministry. They had another refilling with the power of Holy Spirit not so long after: "And when they had prayed, the place was shaken where they were assembled together; and they were all filled with the Holy Ghost, and they spoke the word of God with boldness" (Acts 4:31). We get baptized in the Holy Spirit once but refilled multiple times. We witness that the early Apostles were filled with the Holy Spirit time and again. For example, Peter addressed the Rulers and elders filled with the Holy Spirit (Acts 4.8). Saul, who was also called Paul, filled with the Holy Spirit, looked straight at Elymas (Acts 13.9-11). Stephen, full of the Holy Spirit, looked up to heaven and saw the glory of God, and Jesus standing at the right hand of God. (Acts 7.55). We also need refilling in the Holy Spirit constantly.

The coming of the Holy Spirit brought revolutionary change to the ministry of the apostles. The whole city of Jerusalem was impacted by the move of the Holy Spirit, the Gospel was preached with power and authority, and the sick were healed. Demons were even driven out. The religious and political leaders of the time were worried about the things the Holy Spirit was doing in the hands of the disciples in the city of Jerusalem. However, the power of God continued to extend beyond Jerusalem to neighboring regions such as Judea, Samaria, Gaza, and Joppa. We witness the fulfillment of Jesus's command to his disciples to wait in Jerusalem: "But you will receive power when the Holy Spirit comes on you; and you will be my witnesses in Jerusalem, and in all Judea and Samaria, and to the ends of the earth" (Acts 1:8).

My own personal life and ministry took a radical turn after I was baptized in the Holy Spirit during a Friday evening university student fellowship in July 1993. When the preacher laid his hands upon me for the baptism of the Holy Spirit at the service, I was baptized with the mighty power of the Holy Spirit and spoke in a new tongue for the first time.

My experience with the Holy Spirit continued to grow and expand as I spent more time reading the word and in prayer. A few months after I was baptized in the Holy Spirit, a Christian brother asked me to pray for the baptism of the Holy Spirit for him during a prayer meeting at my dormitory. Three other brothers were praying with us. As I laid my hands on him, the mighty Spirit of the Lord fell on all of us. We all fell to the floor under the mighty power of the Holy Spirit. We could not bear the tremendous power of the Holy Spirit on our physical bodies. None of us were conscious of what happened next.

Later on, we were told that the power of the Holy Spirit shook the entire four-story resident building. Everyone in the building, including the students and housing administrators, ran out of the building to escape the trembling, which, lasted for about 10 minutes. By the time I regained consciousness, the brother I prayed for had received the baptism in the Holy Spirit. He was shaking and praying so loudly in a new language that I asked him to lower his volume in Jesus name. The other brothers were lying on the floor unconscious.

Meanwhile, I heard the voices of a crowd outside the building. When I opened the window and looked outside, the university housing administrators and students cried out to me, "Hurry up; get out of the building. It is an earthquake!" I told them, "It is not an earthquake; it is the Holy Spirit's power that shook the building! Our God is so powerful that he can shake everything." The fear of the Lord came upon them as I spoke to them. A few students who were mean to me because of my faith in Jesus Christ have been respectful, and even some of them became believers. It was a refilling moment in the Holy Spirit for me.

The anointing began to make a difference far beyond the university campus. Days later, I went to visit my siblings on the other side of the city of Addis Ababa,

Ethiopia. They were in the middle of practicing traditional idol worship when I arrived at their house. The witchdoctor, barely visible because of incense smoke, was sitting in the middle of the room and was in the middle of his ritual, which involved praising, singing, and at times groaning and screaming. I sat in the corner of the room and kept watching all of his activities. Moments later, the witchdoctor said, "The spirit cannot fully manifest because somebody he does not like is in the house." The witchdoctor demanded that person should leave. Unsurprisingly, the person the witchdoctor's spirit had issue with was me. The witchcraft spirit did not like me because of the presence of the Spirit of God. The devil knows that the same anointing on Jesus is upon his children. We are Jesus's arms and legs on the earth, we are Christ's ambassadors, and we are representing God's interests on earth.

The witchdoctor pointed his finger at me and said, "You should leave the house now." I told the spirit behind the witchdoctor, "You, devil, it is you who is going to leave! I was raised in this house; this place belongs to me, not to you." I felt the power of God blanketed all over me. I stood up and commanded the witchcraft spirit to leave the house in the name of Jesus Christ of Nazareth.

The witchdoctor fled the house. My siblings were utterly shocked to see Jesus' victory over the devil, and the host of the traditional worship accepted Christ as her savior that day. Praise the Lord! The devil recognizes the anointing upon God's people and cannot do his business as usual in the presence of the anointing of God. But you must expect some challenges from the devil because he always tries to discourage anointed people from doing God's work. So many servants of God yielded to the devil's call to quit; however, we have to realize that the devil is a defeated foe. He can only bark, not bite. I once heard someone say that the devil is a toothless dog that only barks. Jesus took all authority from the devil and gave it to us. Therefore, never give the devil a foothold. As the saying goes, if you give the devil an inch, he wants to become a ruler. The Bible tells us to "resist the devil, and he will flee from you"

(James 4:7). The devil does not deserve an inch of God's promise to His children.

Chapter Two: Igniting the Spiritual Gifts

The Holy Spirit did not come to the disciples with empty hands on the day of Pentecost; He brought along a package of gifts. The Bible refers to them as spiritual gifts (1 Corinthians 12:1). The apostle Paul explains the gifts as follows.

"Now there are diversities of gifts, but the same Spirit. For to one is given by the Spirit the word of wisdom; to another the word of knowledge by the same Spirit; to another faith by the same Spirit; to another the gifts of healing by the same Spirit; to another the working of miracles; to another prophecy; to another discerning of spirits; to another divers kinds of tongues; to another the interpretation of tongues: But all these works that one and the selfsame Spirit, dividing to every man severally as he will" (1 Corinthians 12:4-11).

Beloved Bible teachers Howard Carter and Lester Sumrall divided those nine gifts of the Spirit into three major clusters. The first cluster is what they called the "gifts of revelation." These include the word of wisdom, word of knowledge, and the discerning of the Spirit. "The gifts of revelation" have been commonly manifested in the Prophets office. The second cluster is called "the gifts of power," which includes the gifts of faith, gifts of healings, and the working of miracles. The third cluster is called "the gifts of utterance." This cluster includes prophecy, speaking in tongues, and the interpretation of tongues.

However, it is worth noting that even though all of the gifts of the Spirit have the same origin, the Holy Spirit, operates each distinctively. They never overlap with each other, but they work together very closely. With the exception of speaking in diverse tongues and the interpretation of tongues, the rest of the gifts of the Spirit have been operating both in the Old and New Testaments. The gift of tongues and the interpretation of tongues are given only to the New Testament believers.

The Bible warns us not to be ignorant about those gifts of the Spirit. In his first letter to the Corinthian Church, the Apostle Paul emphasized the significance of the gifts of the Spirit. He said, "Now concerning spiritual gifts, brethren, I would not have you ignorant" (1 Corinthians 12:1). To be ignorant simply means to be without knowledge of something that exists. The Bible clearly underscores that lack of knowledge could cause terrible destruction to lives. "God says my people are destroyed from lack of knowledge" (Hosea 4:6). Ignorance is one reason for the lack of knowledge. For instance, many times we fail to recognize the terms and conditions stated on the contract of a credit card or loan, and as a result we end up paying more fines. It cannot be the company's fault. It is primarily our fault for not paying the necessary attention before we sign the contract. In the same way, some of us live below God's greater spiritual, economic, and intellectual potentials because we fail to pay attention to details about God's prescriptions for our lives.

God gave us the spiritual gifts to bring holistic victory and prosperity to our life. Now to each one the manifestation of the Spirit is given for every man to benefit him (1 Corinthians 12:7). The benefit is for all believers. The gifts are free. They cannot be earned. They are given to us because of the grace of God. These gifts are given to successfully advance God's purpose in our lives and ministry, and serving with the gifts of the Spirit is a privilege, not a right.

Though gifts are given to us, they still belong to God. They operate only at the will of the Holy Spirit. They can be taken away from us anytime; they are not personal property. They cannot be used for personal enrichment. Some ministers couldn't last in the ministry of the gifts of the Spirit because they tried to abuse their responsibility to God. They started humble but grew to become prideful, and God does not tolerate anybody who tries to share his glory. He will have patience with pride for a while to give a chance for repentance, but he will ultimately take away the privilege if pride continues. The devil was disgraced because of his pride. As James 4:6 tells us, "God opposes the proud but shows favor to the humble."

The apostle Paul reminded his spiritual son, Timothy, not to neglect the Spiritual gifts (1 Timothy

4:14). He should rather stir up the gift of God (2 Timothy 1:6). Do you know every Spirit-filled believer has received gifts from the Holy Spirit? Only those who unwrap the gift would know what kind of gift(s) he or she has received. So, have you opened the gifts and enjoyed them yet? If not, it is time to unwrap the package! Do not wait any longer. It is time to rediscover what is in store for you.

As a young farm boy, I used to watch my mother putting extra wood into the fire every night to keep the fire burning through the night. We did not have matches or lighters in those days. If mother did not do that every night, we will be cold and in darkness throughout the night, and there would be no fire for the next day. If we neglect the gifts of the Spirit, we would live in a spiritually dark and cold place. The gifts of the Spirit are like the matchsticks. If you do not strike them, they do not ignite. Let us look at nine of the gifts of the Spirit one-by-one: (1) the word of wisdom, (2) the word of knowledge, (3) the discerning of spirits, (4) the gift of faith (forceful faith), (5) the gift of healing, (6) the working of miracles, (7) the gift of prophecy, (8) speaking in diverse tongues and (9) interpretation of tongues.

Chapter Three: The Gift of the Word of Wisdom

Now there are diversities of gifts, but the same
Spirit.... For to one is given by the Spirit the word of
wisdom (1 Corinthians 12:1, 4, 8).

The gift of the word of wisdom is one of the
revelation gifts of the Holy Spirit and manifests when
the Holy Spirit reveals God's will and purpose about
the future. Through the gift of the word of wisdom,
the Holy Spirit reveals to us what to do, how to do it,
and where and when to carry out a specific
assignment.

The Gift of the Word of Wisdom vs General Wisdom

There is confusion between the gift of the word of
wisdom and general wisdom; they are two different
things. We receive general wisdom when we ask the
Lord in prayer to give us wisdom about decisions to
make or actions to take in our daily lives. For
example, James writes, "if any of you lacks wisdom,
you should ask God, who gives generously to all
without finding fault, and it will be given to you"
(James 1:5). This is what is known as a general

wisdom, which we get by asking God to give us His guidance on the matter at hand.

On the other hand, the word of wisdom is not something we request and receive. The Holy Spirit takes the initiative to give us wisdom. In other words, this wisdom comes as a gift from the Holy Spirit when we have no idea about what is to come.

Another example about the general wisdom is King Solomon's wisdom.

King Solomon asked God, "Give me wisdom and knowledge, that I may lead this people, for who is able to govern this great people of yours?" God said to Solomon, Since this is your heart's desire and you have not asked for wealth, possessions or honor, nor for the death of your enemies, and since you have not asked for a long life but for wisdom and knowledge to govern my people over whom I have made you king, therefore wisdom and knowledge will be given you. And I will also give you wealth, possessions and honor, such as no king who was before you ever had and none after you will have" (2 Chronicles 1.10-12).

According to this example, King Solomon asked God for a general wisdom of administration to rule over Israel. God granted him his request because as James wrote, "God gives so generously to anybody who asks for His wisdom"

We can ask God for general wisdom to excel in our profession, school, business, raising children, or not to make poor decisions. I remember my wife asking God for His wisdom to have her own patents as an electrical engineer, and God gave her some engineering ideas some years later. Now she does have not one but two patents under her belt. Praise God! I believe that all scientific discoveries, technological innovations, and medical miracles are results of God's general wisdom imparted to human minds for the benefit of humanity because of His mercy.

The Gift of the Word of Wisdom vs Prophecy

The gift of the word of wisdom has been greatly misunderstood with the gift of prophecy. The gift of word of wisdom enables the recipient of the gift to see the future, whereas the gift of prophecy serves to renew or re-energize a person who is currently sad, broken hearted, or lonely because of past negative experiences or fear for the future.

According to 1 Corinthians 14:3-4, the Bible says prophecy has three purposes: edification (strengthening); exhortation (encouraging); and comfort (mending the broken heart). Clearly, the purpose of prophecy is not to predict the future but rather to restore, encourage, and bring healing to an individual and the Church.

God may reveal a message of warning, judgment, and even death through the gift of the word of wisdom. For example, the gift of the word of wisdom was in operation when Peter said to Ananias's wife, "Behold, the feet of them which have buried thy husband are at the door, and shall carry thee out. Then fell she down straightway at his feet, and yielded up the ghost: and the young men came in, and found her dead, and, carrying her forth, buried her by her husband" (Acts 5:9). That was not prophecy because the message Peter gave was neither edification, nor exhortation, nor comfort; it was the message of God's judgment. Peter was led by the gift of the word of wisdom in this particular case.

As for the gift of prophecy, the Holy Spirit reminds us of God's already established covenant to edify, exhort, and comfort us. In other words, the Holy Spirit reassures that we have God's sovereign provision of safety, security, and protection amid difficult situations. For example, David prophesies about the established protection and provision of God in his Psalm 23 and Psalm 91. In these sections of his song, David reminds himself that God is in full control under any circumstance.

In the New Testament, Jesus has given comforting (prophetic) messages many times. For example, Jesus gave a prophecy about not being troubled because God has already prepared a place for us (John 14:1). (More illustrations about the gift of prophecy are in chapter nine.)

It is important to note that the prophet (the person in the office of prophet) predicts the future with the gift of the word of wisdom, not with the gift of prophecy. The prophet may have both the gifts of the word of wisdom and of prophecy jointly operating in his or her ministry. Moses operated in the gifts of the word of wisdom and prophecy when he spoke to the Israelites before they left Egypt: "Do not be afraid. Stand firm and you will see the deliverance the Lord will bring you today. The Egyptians you see today you will never see again" (Exodus 14:13).

"Do not be afraid" is the prophetic portion of Moses's statement. "Stand firm and you will see the deliverance the Lord will bring you today" is the portion of the word of wisdom. If the prophet gives prediction about the future, he is not operating in the gift of prophecy. Instead, he is operating in the gift of the word of wisdom because prediction is involved in his message.

Another example of the word of wisdom is in Acts 21:10-11: "After we had been there a number of days, a prophet named Agabus came down from

Judea. Coming over to us, he took Paul's belt, tied his own hands and feet with it and said, 'The Holy Spirit says, "In this way the Jewish leaders in Jerusalem will bind the owner of this belt and will hand him over to the Gentiles." Prophet Agabus foretold what was going to happen to Paul in Jerusalem with the gift of the word of wisdom. The prophet's message was not prophetic in nature because the message did not contain comforting message to Paul.

The Word of Wisdom in Old Testament

There are many Old Testament accounts of gifts of the word of wisdom. For example, Joseph had a gift of the word of wisdom.

Joseph had a dream, and when he told it to his brothers, they hated him all the more. He said to them, "Listen to this dream I had: We were binding sheaves of grain out in the field when suddenly my sheaf rose and stood upright, while your sheaves gathered around mine and bowed down to it." His brothers said to him, "Do you intend to reign over us? Will you actually rule us?" And they hated him all the more because of his dream and what he had said (Genesis 37:5-8).

God revealed to Joseph through the gift of the word of wisdom about what was going to happen to him and his brothers ahead of time. Indeed, his brothers bowed before him after nearly 15 years in Egypt.

Joseph had another word of wisdom when he interpreted Pharaoh's dream. "Joseph said to Pharaoh, the seven good cows are seven years, and the seven good heads of grain are seven years; it is one and the same dream. The seven lean, ugly cows that came up afterward are seven years, and so are the seven worthless heads of grain scorched by the east wind: They are seven years of famine" (Genesis 41.26). The seven years of abundance in Egypt came to an end, and the seven years of famine began, just as Joseph had said. There was famine in all the other lands, but in the whole land of Egypt there was food. When all Egypt began to feel the famine, the people cried to Pharaoh for food. Then Pharaoh told all the Egyptians, "Go to Joseph and do what he tells you"

(Genesis 41. 53-55). Here again the events God revealed to Joseph through the gift of the word of wisdom had come to pass.

There are many more Old Testament examples of the manifested word of wisdom in the lives of the kings, prophets, and priests, including the word of wisdom in the ministry of the prophet Elisha. It was he who announced, "Hear the word of the Lord. This is what the Lord says: 'About this time tomorrow, a seah of the finest flour will sell for a shekel and two seahs of barley for a shekel at the gate of Samaria.' …. So a seah of the finest flour sold for a shekel, and two seahs of barley sold for a shekel, as the Lord had said" (2 Kings 7:1-20).

The Word of Wisdom in the New Testament

In the New Testament, the gift of the word of wisdom has manifested in the ministry of our Lord Jesus Christ and His disciples on numerous occasions. For example, Jesus said to the blind man, "Go, wash in the Pool of Siloam." So the man went and washed and came home seeing (John 9:7).

Before His crucifixion, Jesus told Peter, "Before the rooster crows today, you will deny three times that you know me" (Luke 22:34). Then Judas, the one who would betray him, said, "Surely you don't mean me, Rabbi." Jesus answered, "You have said so" (Matthew 26:25). Jesus had foretold that Judas would hand him over to the Pharisees

Many manifestations of the word of wisdom appear in the ministries of the apostles and other believers. For example, Apostle Paul understood the coming of a shipwreck before they sailed off across the Mediterranean Sea. So Paul warned them, "Men, I can see that our voyage is going to be disastrous and bring great loss to ship and cargo, and to our own lives also." But the centurion, instead of listening to what Paul said, followed the advice of the pilot and of the owner of the ship (Acts 27:9-10). After they had gone a long time without food, Paul stood up before them and said: "Men, you should have taken my advice not to sail from Crete; then you would have spared yourselves this damage and loss. (Acts 27.21)

The Consequences of Ignoring the Word of Wisdom

The Holy Spirit gives the gift of the word of wisdom for our benefit. God's wisdom is vital for right living, and that is why some believe this is the greatest of all of the gifts of the Spirit. The word of wisdom protects us from taking wrong directions or making wrong decisions and brings us in line with God's future plans for our lives. However, if we do not take the word of wisdom seriously, we can expose ourselves to physical, mental, emotional, and spiritual destruction. For example, Jesus spoke a word of wisdom to a young rich man what to do for the rest of his life. Sadly, the young man ignored God's wisdom for his life. Jesus said to him, "If you want to be perfect, go, sell your possessions and give to the poor, and you will have treasure in heaven. Then come, follow me. When the young man heard this, he went away sad because he had great wealth" (Matthew 19:21-22). As Jesus said, "What good will it be for someone to gain the whole world, yet forfeit their soul? Or what can anyone give in exchange for their soul?" (Matthew 16:26). If we ignore the word of wisdom we expose ourselves to lose our rights. We may open ourselves to personal crisis such as, debts, early death, bondage, wrong marriage and relationships, and failure in our ministry.

Personal Experiences with the Word of Wisdom

The Holy Spirit has communicated with me through the gift of the word of wisdom on a number of occasions. Here are selected ones.

Early in my Christian days, the Spirit of the Lord spoke to me as I was heading out of my house to do some shopping downtown. The Spirit of the Lord suddenly whispered to me the name of a person I would meet on my way. A few blocks later, I saw the same person coming towards me. Some may wonder about the Lord mentioning someone's name, but the Lord knows us by name; He knows everything about us, inside and out.

Word of Wisdom about Family

My wife, Mulu, and I were doing our morning devotional when the Spirit of God gave me the word of wisdom about our babysitter. The Spirit told me "the babysitter will be late because of heavy traffic caused by an accident ahead of her." A few minutes after prayer, the babysitter called to inform us that she was going to be late because of traffic. She mentioned that an accident caused the delay.

One day, a Christian brother and I were praying at my office. I heard from the Spirit of the Lord that his wife was a few weeks pregnant and she would be having a baby girl. Immediately, I shared with him what the Lord had just revealed to me. Two months later they found out that they were expecting a baby girl!

Another day, I was urged by the Spirit of the Lord to make a call to my brother Getahun who lives in Auckland, New Zealand. Somebody answered his cell phone and said, "Your brother has suffered a massive stroke and is now in a coma. The doctors do not expect him to survive." My brother was only 26 years old at the time. Obviously, I was devastated by the news. Later the day, I was lying on my bed. In a vision, I saw myself and my brother standing together on the top of a high ground. I heard the Spirit of the Lord saying to me, "Your brother will live." My brother spent two years in rehabilitation centers and had to learn to do everything all over again. His spiritual life took a new turn for good, and a few years later, he got his masters in science and got married and now is raising two great kids. As the Lord had shown me in the word of wisdom, so it came pass.

In 2014, the Lord gave me a message of warning to a young man who was living in the US. I immediately contacted his parents and told them the message from the Lord. Unfortunately, the young man passed away in a tragic car accident less than a year later.

Baptism in the Holy Spirit

While walking on the campus of Oral Roberts University in Tulsa, Oklahoma, my brother-in-law and I were talking about some personal and family issues; all of a sudden, I heard the Spirit of the Lord say to me, "Your brother-in-law does not need to worry about a thing. He only needs to receive my power. Take him to the Prayer Tower." The Prayer Tower is located at the center of the University, which was a few thousand feet away from where we were. After we checked into one of the prayer rooms inside the Prayer Tower, I laid my hands on him, and the power of the Holy Spirit came upon him so mightily. He was baptized with the Holy Spirit and spoke in new tongues for the first time. Because of the mighty manifestation of the Holy Spirit, so many people in the prayer rooms came out to check on us. I had to ask the Lord to turn the power down a bit to give others the privacy they needed. You see how the Holy Spirit changed the direction of our conversation; He knows what is most important for us.

Word of Wisdom for a Gospel Singer

Once I had a dream about an international Gospel singer from another country who happened to be playing soccer with me in Tulsa, Oklahoma. The Lord showed me in a dream that the light went off while he was singing on the stage at a church in California. I prayed about it first. But the Lord said, "Tell him the dream." I did not want to tell him because I did not want to discourage him with a negative message. Again, the Lord spoke to me a week later, urging me to tell him the dream. Still I did not want to tell him because of the respect I have for that singer. On the third week, the Lord spoke to me again saying, "Solomon, if you do not tell him the dream, not only will I no longer trust you, but the blood of my son is upon your hands." It was at this time that I knew something serious was going to happen. I immediately pulled him outside of the soccer field and told him what the Lord had told me. The singer appeared as if he had no clue what the dream might be about. Anyway, I encouraged him to pray about it and went on playing soccer. Two weeks later, I heard that the singer had been asked to leave the U.S. because of his illegal immigration status. He left the U.S. three weeks later. Had I waited any longer, he could have been jailed and deported.

If God gives you a word of wisdom for somebody and you fail to inform that person, you are answering to God. It is always good to pray for that person. Sometimes what the Lord shows and asks us to do may seem illogical, but we should not reason with the Lord about it. We should tell the person with love and respect. The Lord will make a way for you to deliver His message.

Word of Wisdom about Leadership

Let me add one more of my experiences in the Word of Wisdom related to church leadership. I was a leader and member of the Midwest Fellowship of Christian Churches representing a local church the Lord asked me to plant in Tulsa, Oklahoma. In a dream, the Lord showed me a dead person covered in a white sheet. The body was surrounded by the Midwest Christian Fellowship Pastors. The Lord spoke to me in an audible voice, "Do you see the human body lying in the middle?" I answered, "Yes, Lord." The Lord said to me, "That is the body of one of the Midwest Christian Fellowship pastors." A month later one of the pastors was dead, and a month after that another pastor died. The second pastor's death was announced on the day of the Midwest Christian Fellowship's annual gathering in Missouri in 2016.

At another time, the Holy Spirit spoke to me while on the elevator going to my office. He told me that the person who was in the elevator with me (who was also a professor) was going to be the next academic dean of the college. I called my wife and told her what the Lord had told me. I was aware that my university was searching for a new dean to replace the one who had resigned, but I was not aware that this person was interested or had applied for the position. A week later, the search committee announced the names of individuals who were short-listed for an interview, and the name of the person the Lord had given me was listed as one of them. As part of the selection process, each academic department gave their votes. I did not vote in favor of the person the Lord had told me would be the next dean of my college. A few weeks later, the university president announced that the same person the Holy Spirit had told me was appointed as a dean of my college.

You see, God's plan will always prevail even if His servants do not agree with Him. After God rejected King Saul to be a king over Israel, God gave the prophet Samuel a word of wisdom about anointing the next king of Israel from one of Jesse's sons in Bethlehem. However, Samuel replied, "King Saul will kill me if he hears I am going to anoint a new King" (1 Samuel 16:2). Clearly, Samuel disapproved of God's plan, but God insisted Samuel should go ahead to anoint one of Jesse's sons. After Samuel obeyed, Jesse became another obstacle to God's will by not including his youngest son, David, among the potential candidates to be anointed as the next king of Israel. But God had chosen David even though he was not in the mind of Jesse or of the prophet

Samuel. This shows us that no political, spiritual, or social authority can ever stop the will of God happening in our lives. If God declares it, it is for sure going to come pass.

One day, I was walking to my office on the campus of the prestigious University that I was working with as a full professor. The Spirit of the Lord made me aware the name of the next president of the University. The Spirit said the next president of this University is going to be Dr. X (the name of the person is kept confidential). I had not been aware of that name before; however, I knew that the University had been searching for a new president for quite some time. I was also aware that many people had applied for the position. I shared what the Lord said to my wife a few minutes after the Lord spoke to me. Two months later, the University Board announced that the next President would be the same name the Holy Spirit told me.

Chapter Four: The Gift of the Word of Knowledge

Now there are diversities of gifts, but the same Spirit to another the word of knowledge by the same Spirit (1 Corinthians 12:1, 4, 8).

God is omniscient. That means he is all-knowing. God knows about everything, whether visible or invisible, and He knows everything and everywhere in the universe. Everything is before the sight of God.

One of the ways God reveals His knowledge about the past or present situation is through the gift of the word of knowledge, which is one of the revelation gifts of the Holy Spirit: "To another, the word of knowledge by the same Spirit" (1 Corinthians 12:8). We only acquire knowledge from God as He wills. He gives us the word of knowledge about a specific fact or event of the past or present circumstances if He wills to do so.

The word of knowledge does not predict future circumstances. The Holy Spirit reveals though this gift about past and ongoing situations. As previously said, the Holy Spirit reveals future circumstances through the gift of the word of wisdom not through the gift of the word of knowledge; however, the word of knowledge and the word of wisdom work very closely together. The gift of the word of knowledge gives understanding about the root of the problem, whereas the gift of word of wisdom gives understanding about the solution to the problem. The word of knowledge reveals the past and current situation while the word of wisdom gives us God's insight into how to move forward to resolve the situation.

The knowledge that is gained through the academic or scientific research processes is not considered a knowledge gained through the gift of the word of knowledge. The source of the gift of the word of knowledge is the Holy Spirit. The Bible says, "But all these works that one and the same Spirit, dividing to every man severally as He will" (1 Corinthians 12:11). We cannot have the gift of the word of knowledge through intellectual ability. We cannot receive the word of knowledge through our natural or physical abilities. Our physical sense organs such as hearing, sight, taste, touch, and smell are not useful tools to use the supernatural gifts of the word of knowledge.

We cannot get the gift of the word of knowledge through reading the Bible or through theological understanding of the word of God. The word of knowledge is a special gift of revelation when the Holy Spirit make a special move over our Spirit.

The Word of Knowledge in the Old Testament.

The word of knowledge was used during the Old Testament. For example, the blind prophet, Ahijah, recognized King Jeroboam's wife through the gift of the word of knowledge.

At that time Abijah son of Jeroboam became ill, and Jeroboam said to his wife, "Go, disguise yourself, so you won't be recognized as the wife of Jeroboam. Then go to Shiloh. Ahijah the prophet is there—the one who told me I would be king over this people."…. So when Ahijah heard the sound of her footsteps at the door, he said, "Come in, wife of Jeroboam" (1 Kings 14:1-6).

Elijah caught his servant Gehazi accepting unauthorized gifts through the gift of the word of knowledge.

Elisha asked him, "Where have you been, Gehazi?" "Your servant didn't go anywhere," Gehazi answered. But Elisha said to him, "Was not my spirit with you when the man got down from his chariot to meet you? Is this the time to take money or to accept clothes—or olive groves and vineyards, or flocks and herds, or male and female slaves? Naaman's leprosy will cling to you and to your descendants forever." Then Gehazi went from Elisha's presence and his skin was leprous—it had become as white as snow (2 Kings 5:13-27).

The Word of Knowledge in the New Testament

Jesus operated in the gift of the word of knowledge when He told the Samaritan woman about her past and present. Jesus said to her, "You are right when you say you have no husband. The fact is, you have had five husbands, and the man you now have is not your husband. What you have just said is quite true" (John 4.17).

A disciple named Ananias was led by the gift of the word of knowledge to find Saul.

In Damascus there was a disciple named Ananias. The Lord called to him in a vision, "Ananias!" "Yes, Lord," he answered. The Lord told him, "Go to the house of Judas on Straight Street and ask for a man from Tarsus named Saul, for he is praying." …Then Ananias went to the house and entered it. Placing his hands on Saul, he said, "Brother Saul, the Lord— Jesus, who appeared to you on the road as you were coming here—has sent me so that you may see again and be filled with the Holy Spirit" (Acts 9.10-19).

The apostle Peter was made aware of the visitors from Joppa by the gift of the word of knowledge.

While Peter was wondering about the meaning of the vision, the men sent by Cornelius found out where Simon's house was and stopped at the gate. They called out, asking if Simon, who was known as Peter, was staying there. While Peter was still thinking about the vision, the Spirit said to him, "Simon, three men are looking for you. So get up and go downstairs. Do not hesitate to go with them, for I have sent them." Peter went down and said to the men, "I'm the one you're looking for. Why have you come?" (Acts 10:1-23).

Personal Experiences in the Word of Knowledge

The Death of a Professor

The Lord told me in a dream about the death of my former colleague who was a professor and chair of department at one of the universities where I had taught in South Florida. I was no longer working at that university because I had moved away to another city about 200 miles to pursue a medical education. The next morning I shared the dream with my wife. I knew the dream was from the Lord, and it weighed heavily on my spirit for a good part of the morning. Around noon I made a call to my former colleague's office to find out if my friend was alright. His secretary answered. I asked her, "Is Dr. X all right? I had terrible dream about him. I saw him dead." The secretary replied, "Wait a minute until I close my door." Back again on the phone her voice was trembling as she said, "Your dream is right. Dr. X committed suicide last night. We cannot discuss the matter publicly until the university officials formally release the news."

Then she asked whether I was a prophet or a professor. Obviously, she did not expect a professor like me to be a religious person in the vast ocean of secularism and skepticism in the academic world. I told her that everybody will face death one day. But what matters the most is where a person is going to spend eternity. Those who accept Jesus and trust Him will have eternal life. "You need to make that choice," I said. She answered, "I will. I will put my trust in Jesus again."

A few months later, I went to visit my former colleagues at that university. By that time, the dream had been widely communicated among my former colleagues. Some of them asked me whether they would live long or die soon. "You predicted the death of our colleague. How about us?" I told them, "I do not know when you are going to die. But one thing I am sure of is that if you die without Jesus, you will be in a terrible place called hell." Some of them were very afraid about what I said.

Shop Robbery

I and a business man were staying at a mutual friend's house overnight in Durban, South Africa. The business man owned many shops. The Lord showed me in a dream that night that a woman was breaking into one of his stationery shops about 400 miles away and taking some goods. The Lord revealed to me that the female was one of the employees at his shop. In the morning, I told the businessman about the dream the Lord had shown me. The businessman called his security services and found out that the shop had indeed been robbed. He was told that the security service was investigating the situation. I described the person who was involved in the robbery, and he was able to identify her. A few weeks later, the police confirmed that the person who robbed the store was the same person I had described to him. The businessman's faith was elevated because of that word of knowledge.

Sickness

The Lord gave me a word of knowledge in a dream about a person who used to live in our area in Broken Arrow, Oklahoma. In a dream the Lord showed me that the person was having excruciating pain on the right side of his body from his shoulder all the way down. In the dream, I saw myself laying my hands on him for his healing. I and my wife prayed for him immediately after the dream. However, in the morning I went to work without checking on this brother. In the afternoon, as I was driving home together with my wife, this brother and his wife were walking on the side of the road very slowly. I stopped the car and lowered the window to speak to him. As they approached us, I told him about the dream. I told him about the pain on his right side. He confirmed that the location of his pain was accurate. I told him, "The Lord showed me about your pain in my dream, and He also showed me that I was laying my hands on you for your healing." He was willing to have me pray for him at his house. I dropped my family off at our place and went to pray for him at his house. All I did was lay my hands on him and rebuke the pain in the name of Jesus of Nazareth. He was instantly healed! He was able to move his right hand up and down and to all other directions. All of the pain in his body vanished at that point.

Healing

I received a word of knowledge during an evening service at a local church in South Africa. As I got to the podium, I heard the voice of the Lord telling me that the lady sitting in the front seat was suffering from a chronic sinus infection. The Holy Spirit said, "Call her out and I will heal her." I called the woman out to the front and asked her if what I heard from the Lord was accurate. Her answer was "Yes." She added that she was going to be admitted to the hospital for a possible surgery the next day. She had noticeable trouble breathing. I asked everybody to stretch their hands towards her as I was praying for her. I rebuked the sickness in the mighty name of Jesus Christ. The woman was healed immediately, and she could breathe easily again. The next day she went for her surgical appointment. The doctors could not find any trace of growth in that particular area of her body, so she did not have to have surgery. Praise God! That same night the Lord spoke to me about a brother who had lost hearing in his right ear. He was suddenly able to hear without laying a hand on him.

A Deeper Word of Knowledge

Some time ago I was away for a four-day academic trip to St. Louis, Missouri. As soon I got home in Tulsa, Oklahoma, I heard the Holy Spirit saying to take my daughter Rhema to the emergency room even though she looked perfectly fine. I tried to ignore the voice; however, the Lord insisted I should take her to the ER. I took her to the ER when I could no longer ignore the voice of God. After doing x-rays, blood test, and the lab work, the ER doctors said that there was nothing wrong with her. They told me to take her back home; however, I refused to take her back home because the voice from inside said no. I decided to keep her at the hospital for another day. They moved her to the children's hospital, but they did not find anything wrong the next day either. I decided to keep her for the third day.

On the fourth day, the x-ray showed that she already had developed severe pneumonia. The Holy Spirit knew the deepest clinical stage of the disease while medical science could not figure it out at the earliest possible stage. The "Spirit searches all things, yes, even the deep things of God" (1 Corinthians 2:10).

As days passed in the intensive care unit, I continued to cry to the Lord. I asked him why my child should suffer from such terrible sickness. Was it because of my sin or that of her mother's? As her situation grew from bad to worse and reports from the doctors only confirmed her deteriorating condition, I bitterly cried inside my car asking the Lord the same why question. At that point, the voice of the Lord came to me. He said, "It is not because of your sin or her mother's sin. The enemy wanted to destroy her because of what she is going to become." The voice from the Lord directed my attention away from accusing myself and the situation of my daughter to fighting the causative agent of the disease - the devil. Right away, I commanded the devil to take his foul and tormenting disease out of my child's body in the name of Jesus Christ! Suddenly, I felt the peace of the Lord came over my heart. At that point, I know the Lord has delivered my child from the snare of the devil. Then, I went home, took shower and headed to work. Hours later, I went back to the hospital. My wife asked me if I notice any change in the room. I told her, "I do not see anything new." My wife told me that her breathing aid were taken off and she has been breathing on her own for a couple of hours now." Rhema told my wife that a man dressed like a doctor walked inside the room and told her, "Rhema everything is going to be alright." He then untied her hands from the bed and took the breathing tubes off her nostril and walked out of her room smiling. My wife was in the bath room at that moment. When the machine sounded alarm at the removal of the breathing tubes, the medical team and my wife rushed to my daughter. They thought my daughter was dead. Instead, they found her sitting and smiling. The doctors ruled out that she did not need the breathing aid any longer. The next day, Rhema was out of the hospital. The doctors feared that she would be permanently disabled or having breathing problem for the rest of her life. However, that never happened. Rhema is a healthy a kid. She is academically smart and a junior cross-country runner. Parise God!

The Word of Knowledge and Discerning of Spirits

The word of knowledge should not be confused with the devil's counterfeit. We know that the devil is an irrational liar who tries to sell sugarcoated, bogus products. The gift of discernment of spirits helps to identify whether spiritual activities are from God or the devil. Anything from the devil faces rejection from our spirit. We feel uncomfortable deep in our spirit about the counterfeit information we received. The gift of discerning of spirits is discussed in the next chapter.

The word of knowledge does not cause division and animosity among brothers. The word of knowledge that results in fights or leads to criminal activities is not from the Holy Spirit; it is of the devil and therefore counterfeit. The spirit that says to divorce your wife or husband is not of God. The spirit that tells us to rob a bank is not God's Spirit. The spirit that tells us to murder is not of God. The Holy Spirit is love. He never puts someone in harm's way. He reveals the truth with love. The gifts of the Holy Spirit are given to build up the body of Christ, not to destroy. The Holy Spirit is a comforter, not a destroyer. The devil is the destroyer. The thief comes only to steal and kill and destroy (John 10.10).

If you feel threatened by the word of knowledge, pray and ask the Holy Spirit about where this message originating from. Sometimes, the devil tries to pose as the Holy Spirit. If we are stopped by a trooper at a certain location, we may call emergency numbers to find out whether the trooper is genuine or fake. The discerning of the spirit enables us to identify the genuine Spirit of God from the fake. You also need to observe the lifestyle of the person who brings the word of knowledge if the person might have covert ambition for bringing the word of knowledge.

The word of knowledge cannot be for sale. Some minsters claim that people can be freed and out of the spiritual bondage if they put a certain amount of money in the offering bucket. God does not sell His gift; it is free of charge for those who trust in the Lord.

The Gifts of Word of Knowledge and Healings

The gift of the word of knowledge can reveal the moment that healing is taking place during services. However, the word of knowledge is not the same thing as a gift of healing; the word of knowledge is a revelation gift, which means the word of knowledge only discloses the certainty of someone being healed. Kathleen Kuhlman was moved by a strong gift of the word of knowledge and could sense the healing taking place at any corner of a big auditorium. The gift of the word of knowledge plays the role of a spokesperson to deliver news about the healing that took place. For example, Jesus told a Roman officer that his son was healed miles away the very moment Jesus gave him the word of knowledge:

The royal official said, "Sir, come down before my child dies." "Go," Jesus replied, "your son will live." The man took Jesus at his word and departed. While he was still on the way, his servants met him with the news that his boy was living. When he inquired as to the time when his son got better, they said to him, "Yesterday, at one in the afternoon, the fever left him." Then the father realized that this was the exact time at which Jesus had said to him, "Your son will live." So he and his whole household believed. This was the second sign Jesus performed after coming from Judea to Galilee (John 4:43-54).

Here I want to share with you an incidence of the word of knowledge revealing the healing that took place during our church service. As we were holding hands and praying during our Wednesday evening church service, the Holy Spirit suddenly gave me a word of knowledge that the person holding my left hand had just received healing from a severe morning headache. The person confirmed that she had been suffering from frequent headaches almost every morning. A week later she testified that she had not had a headache the entire past week. In this case, the word of knowledge helped to transmit the news of a healing.

There are also instances where the gift of the word of knowledge may reveal a sickness in someone's body without sharing any information about the healing of the person. For example, the gift of the word of knowledge may reveal that someone in the congregation has a certain type of cancer in his or her body, it would be misleading to announce that the person is healed from cancer without receiving confirmation through a gift of the word of knowledge. As said above, the gift of the word of knowledge is not a healing gift; it cannot heal anybody. But the gift of the word of knowledge is a healing spokesperson and can only report what has happened.

Under these circumstances, when the gift of the word of knowledge reveals only the existence of a sickness without healing it, we need the gift of the word of wisdom to understand what to do next. We need to operate in the gift of the word of wisdom about whether to lay hands and pray for the person, or the person should repent, or dip himself seven times in the River Jordan like Niemen, or spit in the dust and put the mud in his eyes like Jesus did, or whether the person should seek medical help. We need to listen to the gift of the word of wisdom to do what should happen next.

When I was ministering in New Zealand, I once heard about an incident in which a preacher spoke a word of knowledge about an individual from the congregation regarding the critical stage of his diabetic condition. The message was accurate; the man indeed had a serious case of diabetes. The preacher also announced that the man was healed from the sickness and should throw away all of his diabetic medications. The man agreed to that and dumped his medications. However, the man was rushed to a hospital the next day for skipping his medication. Obviously, the incidence raised questions and suspicions about the preacher's ministry and the credibility of the word of knowledge and gifts of healing. Clearly, the preacher was lacking the gift of the word of wisdom on how to advise the diabetic patient. He was ignorant about the word of wisdom, or perhaps the gift of the word of wisdom hadn't fully developed in him. As previously said, all the gifts of the Spirit are supernatural; they work at the will of the Holy Spirit. If the Giver does not give us the word, we should remain silent. Some ministers guess what is wrong with a person, but their supposed word of knowledge turns out to be false because it is not from the Holy Spirit. This situation often leads to confusion regarding spiritual gifts.

Chapter Five: The Gift of the Discerning of Spirits

"Now there are diversities of gifts, but the same Spirit. .... To another discerning of spirits" (1 Corinthians 12:10).

The gift of the discerning of spirits is one of the revelatory gifts. This gift is a gateway to the spirit realm and gives the ability to identify the presence and activities of the Holy Spirit, human spirit, and angelic spirits—both holy and evil angels.

Discerning the Presence of the Holy Spirit

Through the gift of the discerning of spirits, we can recognize the presence of the Holy Spirit. Jesus saw the Holy Spirit descending on Him in the bodily form of dove (Matthew 3:16). Luke described the manifestation of the Holy Spirit on the day of Pentecost in the form of fire and violent wind (Acts 2:1). In my spirit, I too have felt the presence of the Holy Spirit move during meetings I've been in—a gentle tickle or warmth on my physical body. When the presence of the Holy Spirit is stronger, my physical body trembles under the power of the Holy

Spirit, and my legs fail to carry my body. I usually ask what the Lord wants to do during an encounter like that.

One day I was asked to pray for a bedridden person in Durban, South Africa. The man was nothing but skin and bones. I felt the presence of the Holy Spirit in a heavy way as I stood at his bedside. While I laid my hands on him and prayed, somebody grabbed my legs. I asked, "What is the matter?" It was the pastor who was also invited to pray for the sick. He said, "The house is full of God's glory. We couldn't walk in His presence; we have to walk on our knees." The pastor was able to recognize the presence of the Holy Spirit through the gift of discerning of spirits.

Discerning the Presence of Jesus

The apostle John had the revelation of Jesus through the gift of the discerning of Spirits.

I turned around to see the voice that was speaking to me. And when I turned I saw seven golden lampstands, and among the lampstands was someone like a son of man, dressed in a robe reaching down to his feet and with a golden sash around his chest. The hair on his head was white like wool, as white as snow, and his eyes were like blazing fire. His feet were like bronze glowing in a furnace, and his voice was like the sound of rushing waters. In his right hand he held seven stars, and coming out of his mouth was a sharp, double-edged sword. His face was like the sun shining in all its brilliance. (Revelation 1:12-16)

One night I had a visit from Jesus in a dream in Tulsa, Oklahoma. I saw him at a playground where many kids were playing. A short while later, I felt hungry and went home to eat some food. The Lord followed me and forced his way into my house. I was terrified; I cried out and called the name of Jesus to save me. I dropped to the floor, and He sat on my belly and started to tickle me. His face changed to something beautiful, and I felt like the happiest person on earth. The peace of God overflowed my spirit and soul. I asked Him why He was there alone at the playground, to which He answered, "I do not have a house; please build Me a house." So my wife and I started a fellowship at our house every Saturday. That fellowship grew out of our house and became a local church in Tulsa.

Discerning the Throne of God

The gift of the discerning of spirits helps us to have an open vision of the throne of God. The prophet Isaiah saw the throne of God in the year that King Uzziah died. The prophet says, "I saw the Lord, high and exalted, seated on a throne; and the train of his robe filled the temple" (Isaiah 6:1). The apostle John had the revelation of the throne of God.

At once I was in the Spirit, and there before me was a throne in heaven with someone sitting on it. And the one who sat there had the appearance of jasper and ruby. A rainbow that shone like an emerald encircled the throne. Surrounding the throne were twenty-four other thrones, and seated on them were twenty-four elders. They were dressed in white and had crowns of gold on their heads. From the throne came flashes of lightning, rumblings and peals of thunder. In front of the throne, seven lamps were blazing. These are the seven spirits of God. Also in front of the throne there was what looked like a sea of glass, clear as crystal (Revelation 4:2-6).

Apostle Paul had access to the third heaven through the gift of the discerning of the spirits.

I know a man in Christ who fourteen years ago was caught up to the third heaven. Whether it was in the body or out of the body I do not know—God knows. And I know that this man—whether in the body or apart from the body I do not know, but God knows—was caught up to paradise and heard inexpressible things, things that no one is permitted to tell" (2 Corinthians 12:12-14).

Discerning the Presence of Holy Angels

Many people have witnessed the presence of the holy angels in congregations during services or at other occasions. Others saw angels protecting and delivering messages from the Lord. The angels of the LORD encamp around those who fear him, and he delivers them (Psalm 34:7). I once heard a preacher say an angel was sitting in the congregation and taking sermon notes while the pastor was preaching. Isaiah saw holy angels worshiping God on His throne (Isaiah 6:2), and Ezekiel saw holy angels worshipping God (Ezekiel 1:6). Apostle John had a revelation of holy angels worshiping in Heaven (Revelation 22:8).

Discerning the Human Spirit

The gift of the discerning of spirits reveals thoughts inside the human spirit (heart), whether they are good or bad thoughts. This gift examines what the human spirit harbors, such as love, hate, anger, offense, unforgiveness, bitterness, grudges, resentfulness, lies, kindness, honesty, selfishness, racism, jealously, self-pity, untrustworthiness, cheating, hypocrisy, gossip, corruption, conspiracy, lust, and dishonesty. For example, Jesus detected the thoughts of the Pharisees and the teachers of the law and asked, "Why are you thinking these things in your hearts?" (Luke 5:21-22). At another time, Jesus was aware that His disciples were grumbling, so Jesus asked them, "Does this offend you? (John 6.61). Jesus discerned that His disciples, James and John were angry at the people of Samaria. They asked, "Lord, do you want us to call fire down from heaven to destroy them?" (Luke 9:53-54). Through the gift of the discerning of spirits, the apostle Peter discerned that Ananias and Sapphira had lied to him, so he said, "Ananias, how is it that Satan has so filled your heart that you have lied to the Holy Spirit and have kept for yourself some of the money you received for the land?" (Act 5:3).

Discerning Evil Spirits

Jesus discerned the presence and activities of the devil many times in His ministry. For example, Jesus replied, "I saw Satan fall like lightning from heaven" (Luke 10:18). Jesus turned to Peter and said, "Get behind me, Satan! You are a stumbling block to me; you do not have in mind the concerns of God, but merely human concerns" (Matthew 16:23).

The apostle Paul discerned an evil spirit. "Elymas the sorcerer (for that is what his name means) opposed them and tried to turn the proconsul from the faith. Paul, filled with the Holy Spirit, looked straight at Elymas and said, 'You are a child of the devil and an enemy of everything that is right! You are full of all kinds of deceit and trickery. Will you never stop perverting the right ways of the Lord? Now the hand of the Lord is against you. You are going to be blind for a time, not even able to see the light of the sun'" (Acts 13:6-11). Luke recalls another such incident with the Apostle Paul."

Once when we were going to the place of prayer, we were met by a female slave who had a spirit by which she predicted the future. She earned a great deal of money for her owners by fortune-telling. She followed Paul and the rest of us, shouting, "These men are servants of the Most High God, who are telling you the way to be saved." She kept this up for many days. Finally, Paul became so annoyed that he turned around and said to the spirit, "In the name of Jesus Christ, I command you to come out of her!" At that moment the spirit left her" (Acts 16:16-18).

Personal Experiences in the Discerning of Spirits

One day while I was traveling on a public bus, the person sitting next to me became uncomfortable and agitated. The Holy Spirit made me aware that a demonic spirit was bothering him. I was sitting next to him quietly when moments later he started to yell and yawn. Then he asked the driver to stop the bus and ran out of the bus at a very high speed.

The devil is uncomfortable around the anointing. Demonic spirits lose their ground when they encounter the anointing of God. Even when Jesus did not provoke them, the evil spirits called out, "What do you want with us, Jesus of Nazareth? Have you come to destroy us? I know who you are—the Holy One of God!" (Mark 1:24). They simply cannot stand the presence of God and His anointing.

It was my first day in South Africa as a doctoral student at the University of Natal in Durban. I rented a house about 15 miles from the school. On the very first night I was awakened from deep sleep by the powerful presence of the army of demonic spirits.

They rushed towards me in what appeared to be a fiery chariot. I was on my feet that very same moment and started to rebuke the demonic forces in the name of Jesus before they crashed on me. I saw the demonic forces disperse in different directions. Even though I was asleep physically, my spirit was alert. The Lord told me, "This is a territorial evil spirit who does not want you to live in this place." The devil does not want to recede an inch from his territory. I commanded the evil spirits to leave this area no matter how long they had been ruling the area.

When Jesus came to a new area, He cast out demons, displacing them. One day an evil spirit said, "Jesus I know, and Paul I know about, but who are you?" (Acts 19:15). We have been given authority from God to expand the territory for Jesus and to take it back from the devil. Jesus came to restore human authority over the devil. Some years back a Christian brother pointed to a brother who the devil was afraid of. I told him that the devil is not afraid of any human, but that the anointing on that person was the only reason why the devil could not stand him.

I was once ministering in a foreign country, and as I was preaching, the spirit of the Lord showed me a demon-possessed young woman in the congregation. I stepped down into the congregation and approached the lady while asking the congregation to pray against the demonic spirits. I laid my hands on the young woman and commanded the spirit to come out of her in Jesus' name. But the spirit did not respond. The demon tried to make me doubt the revelation given to me through the discerning of spirits. I held my ground, and for the second time I commanded the spirit to come out of her. Still nothing happened. I commanded the spirit to come out of her in the name of Jesus for the third time. This time the spirit manifested and cried out, "I was going to kill her. I do not want to leave her. This is my home." I commanded the evil spirit to be quiet and leave in Jesus' name. It left.

One Saturday morning while I was praying, the Lord revealed to me a demonic spirit sitting on the head of a young girl about 90 miles away. I asked the Lord what it was, and He replied, "This is a human sacrifice spirit. I want you to travel to the house where that person lives and cast out the demonic spirit. Hurry before it is too late. The evil spirit is going to drive the person to a location to be killed as part of its ritual tomorrow." I knew the person and the house very well, so I immediately took a taxi to a bus station, hopped on a bus, and arrived three hours later. The young girl and her mother welcomed me cheerfully, and everything looked normal in the natural. She was a newly born again Christian, but her mom was not a believer. The girl was smiling and looking happy, but something was wrong in the realm of the spirit. I asked if I could pray for the young girl; she was willing for prayer. Then I laid my hands on her head and commanded, "You deceptive, murdering spirit, come out of her in Jesus' name!" The evil spirit manifested and cried out, "She is mine; I want to kill her tomorrow. She is on schedule to be sacrificed tomorrow." I commanded the spirit to be quiet and come out of her in Jesus' name. The spirit left, and the young girl fell on the ground. When I again laid my hands on the young girl, she was baptized in the Holy Spirit right there and immediately spoke in new tongues. It was a turning point in the salvation of that house. Her mom, dad, and three other siblings got saved because of the deliverance.

One time, I was standing in a queue to get something to eat in Durban, South Africa. As the person in front of me approached the counter to pay for her food, I saw a demonic spirit move out from the cashier and entered the person in front of me in a split second. I walked away from the line, followed the person, and started talking to her. Everything seemed fine with her. I asked if I could come over her house and pray with her family. She agreed. I got to her house later in the evening. I placed my hand on her head and rebuked the demonic spirit. She fell to the ground at that moment. The demonic spirit cried out, and I commanded it to leave her body in the name of Jesus. The evil spirit left.

Also in Durban, there was a young girl whose aunt told me that her niece had not been able to eat or speak for four days because her jaws were locked shut. I was told that she attended church but her parents followed the Hindu religion. Her Aunt told me that many people had come to pray for her, but nothing had happened. I asked her Aunt if those people had prayed in Jesus' name, and she responded, "Yes?" I asked her, "Why didn't something happen when they prayed in the name of Jesus?" I was in a holy anger that the name of Jesus had not done anything for the young woman. I knew the devil was involved, but I was so curious about the kind of devil that was not challenged by the name of Jesus. I asked the aunt to bring the girl and her mother to her house so I could pray for her, but when I saw the girl for the first time, I thought she was lifeless. As I started to converse with the family while the girl was lying on the bed, the Holy Spirit revealed to me that a substance was in the young woman's belly. I asked, "What is that Lord?" He answered, "There's a witchcraft spirit in her belly."

They call it mutee in South Africa. I commanded it to come out of her belly in the mighty name of Jesus. Now, the girl started to wiggle and twist her lower body like a snake. When I commanded the spirit to reveal itself and let the girl talk, the girl opened her mouth for the first time in four days. The spirit said, "I am the spirit of dragon." The spirit admitted to putting mutee in her belly. I asked her aunt to bring me a bowl and then commanded the spirit to spit out the substance within her body. The girl spewed dried blood and tissue. She was delivered!

Chapter Six: The Gift of Faith

There are different kinds of gifts, but the same Spirit distributes them …to another faith by the same Spirit (1 Corinthians 12:4, 9).

The Bible mentions different kinds of faith: natural faith, saving faith, general faith, and the gift of faith. Let us see each of them in some detail.

Natural Faith

Natural faith comes from having faith in the "general truth." General truth refers to the ongoing, divinely established natural cycle of events on a constant basis. For example, every human being has natural faith that the sun is going to rise the next morning. The Bible says God causes the sun to rise on the evil and the good (Matthew 5:45). When we buy winter clothes ahead of time, we are exercising our natural faith. We know that the seasons are following their natural order and that winter weather is around the corner. We prepare for the other seasons accordingly because of our natural faith. Farmers are good examples for practicing natural faith; they know to expect and follow the seasons of sowing and harvesting.

Saving Faith (limited-purpose faith)

Saving faith refers to faith that leads someone to make the decision to accept Jesus Christ as their personal Lord and Savior: "For it is by grace you have been saved, through faith" (Ephesians 2:8). Salvation is God's free gift to humanity, but we have to have faith in God to be saved. One cannot be saved without faith in the Savior. "If you declare with your mouth, 'Jesus is Lord,' and believe in your heart that God raised him from the dead, you will be saved (Romans 10:9). Saving faith is a limited-purpose faith that leads someone to be born again. For example, the only faith the man on the cross with Jesus experienced was saving faith.

Some Jews applied their saving faith after Peter preached on the day of Pentecost. Peter said to them, "Save yourselves from this corrupt generation." Those who accepted his message were baptized, and about three thousand were added to their number that day" (Acts 2:41). We have to recognize that each saved person has saving faith embedded within in him or her, leading them to make a decision for salvation. Saving faith continues to reassure us that we have eternal life in Jesus Christ after we have been born again.

General Faith (multi-purpose faith)

General faith refers to the measure of faith that God has assigned to each believer (Romans 12:3). God gave every believer a portion of faith after they got saved. General faith is a multi-purpose faith that gives believers the ability to have faith among other things in God's Word, faith to be healed, faith in God for answering prayers, faith in the Blood of Jesus, faith to be baptized in the Holy Spirit, faith to operate in the gifts of the Spirit, faith in resurrection, faith to cast out demons, and faith to overcome daily challenges.

Two examples of general faith from the Bible are in the book of James. "Is anyone among you sick? Let them call the elders of the church to pray over them and anoint them with oil in the name of the Lord. And the prayer offered in faith will make the sick person well; the Lord will raise them up. If they have sinned, they will be forgiven" (James 5:14-15). Another example James gives us is "Elijah was a human being, even as we are. He prayed earnestly that it would not rain, and it did not rain on the land for three and a half years" (James 5:17).

General faith is a growing faith. God gives us a measure of faith to start with, and one way of growing our faith is by feeding on the word of God. "Faith cometh by hearing, and hearing by the word of God" (Romans 10:17). When we hear (e.g., feed on) the Word of God, faith starts to grow in us. The word of God has the power to create faith in us, and the more we hear the word of God, the more our faith gets stronger. "Let the word of Christ dwell in you richly" (Colossians 3:16). The word of God is a nourisher of our faith.

The Gift of Faith (forceful faith)

It is important to know that the gift of faith is a supernatural gift of the Holy Spirit. This is not a regular kind of faith; it is an extraordinary faith that the Holy Spirit gives to anybody as He wills. One cannot have the gift of faith through other means such as theological studies or knowledge of the word of God, because the Holy Spirit is the only source of the gift of faith. One can desire to have the gift of faith; however, it is up to the Holy Spirit to give it to whomever He wills.

Even though the gift of faith resides in us, the Holy Spirit still owns it. We are only vessels to channel what the Holy Spirit wants to accomplish at that moment. We cannot be moving in the gift of faith anytime we want. The Holy Spirit must trigger the gift of faith within the spirit man whenever and wherever He desires.

The gift of faith manifests suddenly and forcefully. The gift of faith usually operates for protection from eminent dangers and for provision during critical times. For example, in the Old Testament, Daniel and the three Hebrew men were protected from life-threatening conditions because of the supernatural gift of faith.

The gift of faith is not deterred by ongoing hostilities. Instead it reverses the looming catastrophe. For example, Apostle Paul persuaded the passengers on a wrecked ship to eat amid the fiercest storm.

Just before dawn Paul urged them all to eat. "For the last fourteen days," he said, "you have been in constant suspense and have gone without food—you haven't eaten anything. Now I urge you to take some food. You need it to survive. Not one of you will lose a single hair from his head." After he said this, he took some bread and gave thanks to God in front of them all. Then he broke it and began to eat. They were all encouraged and ate some food themselves" (Acts 27:33-37).

I once heard a testimony about an evangelist who was surrounded by three communist soldiers. As the soldiers threatened to beat him, the evangelist cried out, "Lord I am only one. They are three." The Lord heard the evangelist as he cried out for help. The

Spirit of the Lord descended on the soldiers and knocked them out on the ground. The evangelist was able to walk away to freedom while the soldiers were sleeping.

The supernatural gift of faith brings the dead back to life. For example, the apostle Paul raise a young man named Eutychus, who was sinking into a deep sleep as Paul talked on and on.

When he was sound asleep, he fell to the ground from the third story and was picked up dead. Paul went down, threw himself on the young man and put his arms around him. "Don't be alarmed," he said. "He's alive!" Then he went upstairs again and broke bread and ate. After talking until daylight, he left. The people took the young man home alive and were greatly comforted (Acts 20:9-12).

A great British man of faith, Smith Wigglesworth raised many dead people back to life by the supernatural gift of faith. The gift of faith bulldozes anything stands on the way.

Personal Experiences with the Gift of Faith

One day around 5:00 am, I was praying when the Lord instructed me to get up and go to my brother Getahun's dormitory while both of us were university students. I answered, "Yes, Lord," But when I got there, he and his roommates were not in their dorm. I went to the office of the housing administration to inquire about them and was told that one of the students from my brother's dorm had been sick and was taken to a hospital. I went to the hospital and found my brother and his friends at the emergency room.

One of my brother's roommates, Abraham, had taken an overdose of sleeping medication and was found unconscious after 12 hours in his bed. The doctors could not resuscitate him, and his organs had failed, causing his systems to shut down. I told my brother and his friends to pray immediately and that God would raise him. They were tired and did not have the motivation to pray. Anyway, I laid my hands on him and said, "Abraham, in the name of Jesus Christ of Nazareth, get up!" Abraham opened his eyes immediately. He uttered a word I could not understand, so I put my hand on his mouth and ordered him to be loosed. He then clearly said, "Please give me water; please give me water." I thanked God. The same day, in the afternoon, Abraham was discharged from the hospital, completely well.

During my summer vacation in the year I got saved, I was praying at my parents' home when I sensed the heavy presence of an evil spirit countering my prayers. I continued to resist the evil spirit in the name of Jesus. A few minutes later I was in a fully blown warfare with the evil spirit. The Holy Spirit came to my aid, and the Lord took me in a vision to a box where my mother kept her idols and worship items. I got up, opened the box, and tossed the items in a toilet. Obviously, the devil was mad, but I commanded him not to reveal to my mother what I had done until I left the house. A few weeks later I left for college. However, the day I left the house, my mother got very sick. She had a rash and blisters all over her head. As she always did, my mother went to get her idols in order to seek help. But to her shock, the idols were not there. In those days, we did not have mobile phones nor a direct phone line in our dorms. My father followed me to campus on the next bus to ask if I had tampered with her idols. I was surprised to see him that evening because I had not expected him to come to campus. "Your mom is sick in bed," he announced. "She could not find her idols; have you removed them?" I admitted that I had, which made my father shake in fear. He asked, "What are we going to do now?" I told my father that the devil attacked my mother to take revenge for what I had done. I felt the spirit of faith rising up from within my spirit at that very moment. As my father was standing in front of me, I commanded the devil to leave my mother alone in the name of Jesus of Nazareth. I told my father to go home where he would find my mother completely fine. Father traveled the 90 miles back home and found my mother cooking. You see there is no limitation to the supernatural gift of faith.

Chapter Seven: The Gifts of Healings

"There are different kinds of gifts, but the same Spirit that distributes them…. to another the gift of healing by that one Spirit" (1 Corinthians 12:4, 9).

Divine healing is God's provision. It is God's plan for His children. Jesus said healing is the children's bread. "But Jesus said unto her, 'Let the children first be filled: for it is not meet to take the children's bread, and to cast it unto the dogs'" (Mark 7:27). Children never work to have bread. Their parents provide for them. In the same manner, Jesus paid the price for our healing. The Bible says, "By His wounds you have been healed" (1 Peter 2:24). God made provision for healing, and He paid the full price. His healing fountain never runs out, and His provision is whole and perfect; there is nothing that needs to be added. God is more than willing to heal us because He loves you and me. Jesus is willing to heal you. "A man with leprosy came and knelt before him and said, "Lord, if you are willing, you can make me clean.' Jesus reached out his hand and touched him. 'I am willing,' He said. 'Be clean!' Immediately he was cleansed of his leprosy" (Matthew 8:2-3).

Healing is for us. One of the main missions of the coming of Jesus was to restore healing to our sick bodies. Jesus cares; God even cares for sparrows. So don't be afraid; you are worth more than many sparrows (Matthew 10.31). All we should do is to be in right standing with Jesus.

How to Receive Divine Healings

God's divine healing comes to us in many ways. But the source of healing is one—Jesus. One of God's healing avenues is the Word of God, meaning the word of God has the power to heal. "He sent out his word and healed them" (Psalm 107:20). Jesus spoke a word and the servant of the Roman officer was healed miles away (Matthew 8:13). Every word that comes out of Jesus has the power to heal us physically, mentally, spiritually, socially, economically, and psychologically. The word of God is medicine to our sick bodies. The word of God is like a double-edge sword that can penetrate our visible and invisible bodies to perform healing. As he was preaching, the apostle Paul saw a man ready to be healed and told him to rise up and walk (Acts 14:9). The word of God prepared the man for his healing.

I have heard so many testimonies of healing through Kathleen Kuhlman's radio ministry. People received their healings as they listened to her preaching the word of God. The word of God has the power to displace diseases and sicknesses out of our bodies. There is healing power in the word of God. So many people have been healed as they were listening to the word of God being preached at church or on the radio or TV. I was healed from chronic sinus problems while watching live Christian television. The preacher on television mentioned the name of the sickness and rebuked it in the name of Jesus. I immediately felt fresh air move inside my nostrils and realized that I was instantly healed! I did not need my medications anymore. Praise God forever more.

Divine healings also manifest through various ways of points of contact, both physical and spiritual. For example, the woman with the issue of blood was healed just by touching Jesus' garment. A piece from the Apostle Paul's cloth was used to receive healing. Apostle Peter's shadow was used as a point of contact to heal the sick. The laying on of hands is the most common way of transmitting healing. Jesus used other physical objects such as saliva, dust, water (such as at the pool of Bethesda) as points of contact to heal. Oil and wine have been used to heal the sick. Apostle Paul told Timothy to have some wine to recover from his sickness. In modern days, many people have claimed to receive healing by touching TV screens during prayers. However, it is important to note that the points of contact have no power to heal; it is God who is the source of healing. God declared, "I am the Lord, who heals you" (Exodus 15:26). However, even though God is the one who is healing, He uses these objects at points of contact in the healing process.

Obstacles to Healing

The trouble comes when the emphasis is placed on the point of contact rather than the source of healing, God Himself. The points of contact are like an electric wire; they only transmit power, but they do not have the ability to generate the power of electricity. We often hear men and women of God who are given more credit than God Himself. However, we have to understand that they are only vessels God has used to extend His healing virtue. God is the one who deserves the glory, not men. No men have healing virtue. We need to revere the giver, not the messenger.

The objects used as points of contact are often put up for sale as a source of healing. There have been too many so-called "men of God" selling holy water and anointing oil from certain places on Christian television and radio as a source of healing. God never sells His healing virtue. Holy water and anointing oil can never heal anybody. It is God who works behind those objects to heal the sick. We receive healing through faith in God, not in objects. As Smith

Wigglesworth said, "Preachers who have money on their minds will lose."

Another obstacle to healing is putting our desire to get healed before desiring God. Healing will not come if we place our desire to get healed before God Himself. God is the one who is supposed to be sought after. Jesus often said, "Your faith has made you whole." God meets the healing needs of those who make contact with God through their faith.

Wrong doctrine is another obstacle to receiving healing. Some do not believe God still does the business of healing; instead, they think healing is a thing of the past. Jesus said healing is the children's bread. That means healing is available to all of God's children throughout generations. God never stopped healing.

Facts about Gifts of Healings

The supernatural gifts of healings are manifested at the will of the Holy Spirit. There will be no healing unless the Spirit of God triggers the gift of healing. Even if we have been given the gift of healing, it is up to the Holy Spirit to activate the gift within us whenever He wills. For example, the great evangelist of the 20th century, Oral Roberts said he knew the moment the healing power of God was activated in him. He felt an electric power running down his right arm when the power of God was available to heal. He never laid his hands on a person for more than 15 seconds. He said he even knew that healing was taking place before the person he laid his hands on recognized it because of the presence of the healing power on his arm.

Smith Wigglesworth waited until the healing power came upon him. Sometimes he prayed for hours by a patient's bedside until the power of God came up on him before he laid his hands on the sick. Only God knows the reason for triggering His healing power in a timely manner. My guess is that God wants us to be ready to receive His healing virtue; He never pushes healing upon anybody. Our will needs to be shown to be healed. For example, Apostle Paul laid his hands on the people on the island of Melita because they were willing to be healed (Acts 28:8-9).

If the person is not willing to participate in the healing, there will be no healing. Even Jesus couldn't heal anybody in His hometown because they did not want Him. In Samaria as well, they pushed Him out, so they were not healed.

The only exception when divine healing does not need the cooperation of a sick person is when the person is unconscious. I found that the healing virtue flew out of me when the person needing healing was unconscious or subconscious. Under such circumstances, input from the inflicted is not required. One day my brother was sick due to food poisoning, so his roommates called me to pray for him. He was unconscious when I arrived at his room. I put anointing oil on my hands and laid my hands on him and rebuked the poison out of his body in the name of Jesus. My brother jumped out of his bed in less than five seconds after laying my hands on him. He shouted, "I am healed! I am healed!" He later explained that some kind of warmth ran through him when he was being healed.

On another occasion, I was in my childhood hometown, standing at a pay phone waiting for my turn. Suddenly, a boy had a seizure, which knocked him to the ground where he hit his head. I ran to the boy and laid my hands on his head, all the while rebuking the seizure in the name of the Lord Jesus Christ. Instantly, the seizure left him, and he calmed down.

Usually when the person with the gift of healing lays his hands on or prays for someone, the sick person recovers—even if that person has not been healed despite prayers that were offered numerous times by others in the past. I recommend that the sick should consider attending healing services because of God's special healing gifts are given to men or women of God. Throngs of people came from across the nations and the continents to attend the healing services of the ministries of Alexander Dawie, George and Stephen Jeffrey, John G. Lake, Smith Wigglesworth, Oral Roberts, A.A. Allen, Jack Cole, Kathryn Khulman and Reinhard Bonnke. Extraordinary healings have taken place because of the supernatural gifts of healing. Nonetheless, no one is exempt from being sick, and even great healing evangelists like Oral Roberts and the apostle Paul himself were afflicted by sickness. Being anointed does not mean you do not get sick. Equally, anointed servants of God need to trust in the Lord for their own healing.

Chapter Eight: The Gift of Working of Miracles

Now there are diversities of gifts, but the same Spirit...to another the working of miracles (1 Corinthians 12:10).

God, not men, is the miracle worker. Even anointed men and women of God are not miracle workers; they are only vessels to channel the miracles. Miracles do not happen at the will of men; instead, they are God's designs. Only God knows how miracles work. For example, Mary told the servants at the wedding, "Whatever he says unto you, do it" (John 2:3-4). Jesus instructed them to fill the jars with water. God has unique ways to perform each miracle. He may not do things the same way He has done in the past. For example, the Holy Spirit may instruct you to speak at the object to bring forth the miracle, just as Jesus spoke at objects many times: He spoke to the storm, to the fig tree, to the dead person, etc. At other times, miracles happened when Jesus touched the persons or objects. We need to follow specific instruction from God on how to enforce the miracle under each circumstance.

God uses the gift of working miracles to temporarily disrupt the law of nature with his divine intervention for the purpose of provision, protection, judgment, and warning. However, the divine intervention stops after the situation is fixed. For example, the Red Sea was parted until the Israelites fully crossed. Then the sea was closed again, returning to its natural state by the time the Egyptian army entered the sea.

The gift has been in operation both in the Old and New Testaments. Let us first consider several manifestations of the gifts of working miracles in the Old Testament.

Both Moses and Joshua had the gift of working miracles. God performed a series of miracles through the hands of Moses to deliver the Israelites from Egyptian captivity. He brought all kinds of judgment on Pharaoh—turned water to blood; brought locust, frogs and flies on the land of Egypt; brought darkness during day time; killed the first born of the Egyptians and their livestock (Exodus chapters 7-9). Moses parted the Red Sea through the gift of working of miracles (Exodus 14:21-22), and gift of working miracles became operational when the priests who carried the ark touched the Jordan River with their feet (Joshua 3:15-16).

The gift of working miracles was given to other Old Testament figures too. Elijah parts Jordan River: (2 Kings 2:8), brings fire from heaven (1 Kings 18:38) (2 Kings 1:12), fills an empty jar with oil: (1 Kings 17:14-16), raises a dead boy (1 Kings 17:21-22), stops rain: (1 Kings 17:1), brings rain back: (1 Kings 18:43-45). Elisha parts Jordan River: (2 Kings 2:14), recovers ax head: (2 Kings 6:5-7), uses bear: (2 Kings 2:23-24), Samson kills lion: (Judges 14:5-6), destroys temple towers (Judges 16:26-30), kills with donkey jaw (Judges 15:15). David kills lions, bears, and Goliath (1 Samuel 17:36) (1 Samuel 17:48-50).

Jesus performed multiple miracles during his ministry. His first recorded miracle is Jesus turning water to wine. Even though we think of it as the first miracle, it was not His first. Jesus must have done miracles in Mary's presence prior to asking Him to do miracles in public. For example, Mary knew that Jesus was born miraculously, without a natural father. Mary was well aware of that fact more than anybody else. Later, Jesus raises dead: (Mark 5:38-42), (John 11:43-44), (Luke 7:14-15), calms storm: (Mark 4:37-39), curses fig tree: (Matthew 21:18-19) and walks on water: (Matthew 14:25-26).

Other New Testament miracles include the apostles Peter and Paul raising the dead, among other miracles. Ananias and Sapphira died under the gift of the working of miracles, and Paul did not die after he was bitten by a deadly snake. Creative miracles happen when the gift of working of miracles manifested.

The Gift of Healing vs the Working of Miracles

Miraculous healings are not caused by the gift of the working of miracles; they are caused by the gift of healings. For example, the crippled man at the gate of Solomon's Temple was healed because of the gift of healing not because of the gift of the working of miracles. However, Smith Wigglesworth raised many people from the dead under the anointing of the working of miracles. The gifts of healings and the working of miracles work very closely, but we should not confuse them as one. For example, the gift of healing and the working of miracles work in conjunction when a dead person is raised back to life. The gift of healing deals with the sickness that caused a person to die while the gift of the working of miracles brings life back to the person. The gift of healing works on the physical body, while the gift of the working of miracles brings the person's soul and spirit back to the body. Without the healing of his body, they would soon die again. Miracles occurring during healing services are not the result of the gift of the working of miracles but rather healings manifested when the gift of healing operates, not the working of miracles. Healings are miraculous; indeed, every manifestation of the gifts of the spirit are supernatural miracles, but they differ from the gift of the working of miracles.

One time when my wife and I were on the highway from Miami to Sarasota, Florida, we realized that our car was running out of gas. We had already passed all the exits, and a road sign indicated the next gas station was about 100 miles away. We prayed that the car should make it until we got to the nearest gas station and drove the car for almost 100 miles with the indicator showing the gas tank empty. As we pulled to a gas station in the next city, the car rolled to a stop. This is an example of the gift of working of miracles because a car cannot run for more than 100 miles without gas.

Chapter Nine: The Gift of Prophecy

Now to each one the manifestation of the Spirit is given for the common good... to another prophecy (1 Corinthians 12:10).

The gift of prophecy is one of the supernatural gifts of the Holy Spirit and manifests under extraordinary stimulation of the Holy Spirit. Prophecy is not a product of human will or intellect. When the Holy Spirit induces a prophetic message in our spirit, the pitch of our voice changes from low to high. The Spirit of God takes control of our mind and speech organs while prophesying. It is so forceful that we cannot have control over the words we are to say. The Holy Spirit is in full charge at that moment. However, once the prophetic message has been delivered, a sense of calmness returns to our spirit and body.

The Purpose of Prophecy

The person who prophesies speaks to people to bolster their strength, courage, and comfort (1Corinthians 14:3). The purpose of prophecy is threefold: strengthening, encouraging, and comforting.

We live in a negative world. We may find ourselves under constant attacks from the enemy to discourage us in every possible front. We may suffer loss of beloved ones or a dear friend. We may experience pain due to illness or accident. We may be disappointed in our actions or reactions to others. We may be heartbroken because of separation from or betrayal by a trusted friend or partner. We may face multiple challenges at the same time. We may face a new challenge as soon as we overcome the old one.

Even if we are strong spiritually, we are not immune from negative circumstances that are a consequence of living in a broken world. The Bible gives us numerous accounts of mighty men and women of God encountering periods of discouragement. One of the greatest men of God who ever lived was Abraham. The Bible says that Abraham was discouraged over lack of a child. "After this, the word of the Lord came to Abram in a vision:

"Do not be afraid, Abram. I am your shield, your very great reward." But Abram said, "Sovereign Lord, what can you give me since I remain childless and the one who will inherit my estate is Eliezer of Damascus? You have given me no children; so a servant in my household will be my heir." Then the word of the Lord came to him: "This man will not be your heir, but a son who is your own flesh and blood will be your heir." He took him outside and said, "Look up at the sky and count the stars—if indeed you can count them…. So shall your offspring be" (Genesis 15:1-5).

Jesus warned us of the reality of challenges we face while on this earth. "I have told you these things, so that in me you may have peace. In this world you will have trouble. But take heart! I have overcome the world" (John 16:33).

Prophecy is God's tool to revitalize us. The Holy Spirit brings Godly comfort, encouragement, and restoration through prophecy. Every one of us needs prophecy at one time or another because prophecy empowers us to avoid becoming enveloped in negative circumstances and to stir up our faith to trust in God. Paul encouraged Timothy to think of the prophecy that came for him. He reminded him to continue to fight. "Timothy, my son, I am giving you this command in keeping with the prophecies once made about you, so that by recalling them you may fight the battle well" (1Timothy 1:18). Here we see that prophecy serves as a means to encourage Timothy to move forward.

How Prophecy Manifests

Prophecy may be manifested through visions, images, signs, the word of God, and dreams and even can be delivered by holy angels.

King David uttered a prophetic promise in this song he composed:

I lift up my eyes to the mountains where does my help come from? My help comes from the Lord, the Maker of heaven and earth. He will not let your foot slip. He who watches over you will not slumber; indeed, he who watches over Israel will neither slumber nor sleep. The Lord watches over you. The

Lord is your shade at your right hand; the sun will not harm you by day, nor the moon by night. The Lord will keep you from all harm. He will watch over your life; the Lord will watch over your coming and going both now and forevermore (Psalm 121:1-8).

I once received a prophetic message while listening to a Gospel song. Suddenly I was elevated to a higher ground as I was listening to the comforting words of Scripture in the hymns. The spirit of the Lord began to captivate my spirit. I regained the strength to come out of the discouraging situation at that very moment. Praise God for prophecy!

What Prophecy Is Not

Prophecy does not predict the future. As discussed in chapter three, the Holy Spirit reveals future events through the gift of the word of wisdom. The main purpose of prophecy is to strengthen, encourage, and comfort.

Too often the gift of prophecy is being confused with the gift of the word of wisdom and the gift of the word of knowledge. The gifts of word of wisdom and word of knowledge strictly work within the office of a prophet. Prophets are seers of the past and future through the gift of the word of knowledge and the word of wisdom respectively. When prophets operate in a gift of prophecy, the content of their message is limited to strengthening, encouragement, and comforting—not predicting the future. However, prophets may bring messages that include prophecy, words of wisdom, words of knowledge, and the discerning of spirits all together because of the anointing in the office of the prophet.

You do not have to be in the office of a prophet to prophesy. The gift of prophecy can widely operate among believers who received the gift of prophecy from the Holy Spirit. "Therefore, my brothers and sisters, be eager to prophesy" (1 Corinthians 14:39).

How to Judge Prophecies

Prophecies are subjected to examination. One way of judging the accuracy of prophecy is whether the prophecy that came confirms our present circumstances or not. If the prophecy that comes does not seem to have relevance to our current situation, then its validity is deemed questionable.

A friend of mine once told me about his experience with inaccurate prophecy delivered by a preacher while in attendance at a small group fellowship. The preacher told him that he was sad because his parents were not saved. The preacher reassured him that his parents will be soon saved. However, the preacher did not know that his parents died years before. My friend confronted the preacher because his prophecy was untrue and that it caused him pain. Prophecy is meant to give us hope and encouragement, not to intimidate or destroy us or cause us harm in any way.

We can also judge the accuracy of prophecy through the lens of the word of God. Any prophecy that is contrary to the word of God is a counterfeit. Prophecy is supposed to confirm our covenants and promises we have in God. Any prophecy that contradicts Scriptural truths is destined to the trash can.

Chapter Ten: Speaking in Diverse Tongues and Interpretations

Now there are diversities of gifts, but the same Spirit… to another different kinds of tongues, to another the interpretation of tongues (1 Corinthians 12:10).

Diverse Tongues and Regular Tongues

Speaking in different kinds (diverse) of tongues is an extraordinary linguistic manifestation that only happens when the Holy Spirit triggers it. It may even be a different language—as the Spirit gives it—every time we speak. The gift of speaking in diverse tongues is not the same as the regular speaking in the Holy Spirit language we received during the baptism in the Holy Spirit. Speaking in a diverse tongues is a special gift of the Holy Spirit. The utterance in diverse languages is more forceful than speaking in regular tongues—what Oral Roberts called "the prayer language." The utterance in the languages does not happen regularly. It happens only when the Holy Spirit triggers it.

Regular tongues stay with us all the time. We can speak the language anytime we want like the natural language. Regular tongues bring personal restoration and renewal; whereas, the gift of diverse language brings messages to encourage individuals and the Church as a whole. However, the message in diverse tongues needs to be interpreted to benefit the listeners. The message that is interpreted edifies the Church (1 Corinthians 14:2, 27). If no interpreter is in the church at the time, the speaker should be quiet and pray quietly to God. The speaker may pray to receive the gift of interpretation as well (1 Corinthians 14:13).

Speaking in a regular tongue is a sign of being baptized in the Holy Spirit. It is supernatural because its origin is in heaven. Therefore, trying to speak in the Holy Spirit language is impossible through human intelligence and through natural ways of learning the language. It is the Holy Spirit language. Luke describes the first Pentecost in this way: "Suddenly a sound like the blowing of a violent wind came from heaven and filled the whole house where they were sitting. They saw what seemed to be tongues of fire that separated and came to rest on each of them. All of them were filled with the Holy Spirit and began to speak in other tongues as the Spirit enabled them" (Acts 2:2-4).

Language is one of the features of human identity. There is no nation or tribal group without a language of its own, and it is quite normal for people to identify with others who speak the same language. Those who speak the Holy Spirit language can also identify themselves as having a shared identity with other believers in the Lord Jesus Christ. The Lord Jesus said, "And these signs will accompany those who believe: ...they will speak in in new tongues" (Mark 16:17). Some say that speaking in regular and diverse tongues ceased after the first century Church. However, the gift of speaking in tongues is as active today as it was during the Early Church.

The Purpose of Speaking in regular Tongues

The Holy Spirit gives us this special language to communicate with God individually and as a church. We need to know that speaking in tongues (as in a prayer language) is more than speaking a strange language; it is an honor of speaking to God. The Bible says, "One who speaks in tongues speaks to God" (1 Corinthians 14:28). The more we pray in a Holy Spirit prayer language, the more we find ourselves in line with the will and purpose of God. Apostle Paul writes, "The Spirit helps us in our weakness. We do not know what we ought to pray for, but the Spirit himself intercedes for us through wordless groans. And he who searches our hearts knows the mind of the Spirit because the Spirit intercedes for God's people in accordance with the will of God" (Romans 8:26-27).

It is best to start prayers in the Holy Spirit given language for a number of reasons. First, beginning our prayers in the Holy Spirit language gives the Holy Spirit an opportunity to guide us from the start. He points out to us what to pray about and how to pray at that particular time. We will have a more effective prayer time if we pray in tongues.

Second, beginning our prayers in the Holy Spirit language also prepares the ground for God to speak to us. God communicates His will and purpose through the language of the Holy Spirit.

Third, speaking in regular Holy Spirit language empowers our spirit as we start to pray. "Anyone who speaks in a tongue edifies themselves" (1 Corinthians 14:4). The Holy Spirit builds up our inner person through prayer in tongues. We will soar above the natural circumstances as we continue to pray in the Spirit. I personally get edified when I pray in tongues. I feel all kinds of burdens lifted off my spirit and mind during the course of praying in the Spirit language.

Fourth, beginning our prayers in regular tongues creates an atmosphere for the manifestations of other gifts of the Holy Spirit. I often experience simultaneous manifestations of other gifts of the Spirit—such as the gifts of the word of wisdom, word of knowledge, faith, and discerning of spirit—while praying in tongues.

Speaking in regular tongues is an amazing way of recognizing the wonders of God. People listening to Peter and the other apostles preaching were amazed and said, "We hear them declaring the wonders of God in our own tongues!" (Acts 2:11). Perhaps natural language is not sufficient enough to describe the wonders of God. Only the heavenly language has the ability to describe the supernatural characters of God.

Speaking in regular tongues is a supernatural way of praising God in the Spirit (1 Corinthians 14:16), "for they heard them speaking in tongues and praising God" (Acts 10:46) and thanksgiving to God (1 Corinthians 14:16). When I feel inadequate to thank God in the natural, I pray in tongues to express how grateful I am for what He has done for me. My heart is filled with an incredible joy as the prayer language of the Holy Spirit flows through me.

A Holy Spirit language is a mystery language. For anyone who speaks in tongues does not speak to people but to God. Indeed, no one understands them; they utter mysteries by the Spirit (1 Corinthians 14:2). The devil has absolutely no idea about the content of conversation between God and the speaker. At times, when I was dealing with the demonic spirit-possessed person, I prayed in tongues. The demonic forces cannot stand the power of the presence of God coming through praying in tongues and begs to let him go as soon as possible. When we speak in tongues, we keep the devil at bay.

The Gift of Interpretation

Interpretation deals with converting a message spoken in diverse tongues into another language. The gift of interpretation is not the same as translation. Whereas translation is the process of converting every word into another language, the purpose of interpretation is to accurately pass the message to other people. Translation is done by a linguistic expert; interpretation is the gift of the Holy Spirit. Interpretation may come in the form of words, images, or visions. The interpreter may be given shorter or longer messages than the original messages in diverse tongues. However, it has to be noted that regular Holy Spirit language will not be interpreted. Only the diverse Holy Spirit languages can be interpreted.

The interpretation may start with a few words and develop more fully. Usually the interpreter does not receive the whole length of a message all at once. The interpretation drops into the interpreter's spirit and the whole message may not be revealed until a little later. However, the message expands once interpreter starts to open his or her mouth.

Chapter Eleven: Diverse Callings and the Need for Order

There are different kinds of service, but the same Lord (1 Corinthians 12:5). God calls each of us for a unique assignment. One cannot start a ministry by getting a theological education or because it is a career choice or because of a family tradition or a personal passion for evangelism. It is God who owns the ministry, and He knows where and how we can best fit into the service of his Kingdom. We need to discover our calling by diligently asking the Lord. He is our maker and knows us better than anybody does, just as manufacturers know the products they make.

All of us are not assigned to the same line of duty. Some of us are called to work at the front lines. While others are called to serve behind the scenes. All of us are not called to serve from the pulpit. I observed the burning desire of many members of a small church I planted and pastored to serve. While their willingness to serve was a good thing, many of them wanted to serve only behind the pulpit. One day I had a vision from the Lord. In the vision, the Lord showed me that the members of the church congregated on the pulpit area rather than sitting at the area designated for the regular worshipers in the church. It was difficult to lead under such circumstances where everybody wants to be a preacher or a leader of the church.

We have to know that each of us is called for a unique assignment. As Paul puts it "For just as each of us has one body with many members, and these members do not all have the same function" (Romans 12.4) All of us are important vessels. The Lord expects us to be faithful in every assignment He has entrusted to us, whether small or big: "Whoever can be trusted with very little can also be trusted with much, and whoever is dishonest with very little will also be dishonest with much" (Luke 16:10). God's call may start small. He may expand our service area as we obey Him. I once heard a servant of God ask the Lord in her old age why he had not used her when she was younger and had more physical strength to work for Him. The Lord answered, "I did not trust you back then." Those who say I am too old to be used by the Lord should know that nothing is too late for the Lord.

God never expects us to serve Him like somebody else. I often hear that people ask God to anoint them like such and such men and women of God. But the truth of the matter is that God never anoints anybody like somebody else. He always anoints us with greater anointing than we might think if we believe in God's ability to do it. Therefore, we should not waste our time in coveting the anointing that somebody else gets.

We often witness church and ministry leaders involved in reckless competition, rivalry, and even lawsuits to have victories over one another instead of cooperating with each other. Some became jealous and bitter towards the anointed servant of God. They feel inferior and threatened by the anointing the Lord has entrusted upon his servant. They even form groups within the church in an effort to discourage the servant God uses. However, such moves not only offend the Holy Spirit but their actions can stand on

His way to use them. Needless to say, God has no interest in completion, rivalry and squabble for power and status in His church.

The servants of God also have a responsibility to watch out for "a devil in disguise." God's servants need to hear from the Lord and shouldn't rush to embrace just anybody into the ministry, even their own family members. God's servants have a responsibility to protect the vision they have received from the Lord so they should take proper spiritual measures to protect themselves and the work God has entrusted to them. The servant of the Lord should be aware that the deceiver does not usually come from outside his circle but rather from within. Jesus was handed over by one of His own disciples. Satan deceived Adam through his own wife. The apostle Paul had a good reason for choosing to take Silas instead of Mark on that specific mission recorded in Acts 15:40.

Our Lord Jesus prayed before He selected His Apostles. We should also pray about who should work with us in the service of the Lord. Only those who are confirmed by the Lord should be appointed to a specific church assignment. Others should be encouraged to seek the Lord for vision and direction from the Lord instead of arguing with fellow servants of the Lord.

I have personally learned from my own experiences that hasty appointment of people on service positions causes more harm than good to the work of the Kingdom of God. I should have spent more time praying and knowing the personal life of those individuals and their commitment to the Lord and the vision of the church before embracing them into the ministry. Before appointing someone, the leader of the church or ministry should take the necessary precautions.

Equally importantly, as believers, the first thing we should do is to discover our own place in the service of the Lord. Knowing our place in the service of God normally qualifies us to receive the necessary gifts from the Holy Spirit to effectively carry out the work the Lord has entrusted upon us. The Holy Spirit will not be able to reach us with His gifts if we do not position ourselves at the right place. We are half way to success the moment we discover our place and align ourselves with the Holy Spirit. Obviously, the gifts of the Spirit will flow normally and function fully as we totally align with Him.

Made in the USA
Monee, IL
31 July 2021

74262501R00073